WHY DID ENGLISH SETTLERS COME TO VIRGINIA?

And Other Questions about the Jamestown Settlement

Candice Ransom

LERNER PUBLICATIONS COMPANY · MINNEAPOLIS

A Word about Language
English word usage, spelling, grammar, and punctuation have changed over the centuries. We have preserved original spellings and word usage in the quotations included in this book.

Lerner Publications Company
A division of Lerner Publishing Group, Inc.
241 First Avenue North
Minneapolis, MN 55401 U.S.A.

Website address: www.lernerbooks.com

Library of Congress Cataloging-in-Publication Data

Ransom, Candice, 1952–
   Why did English settlers come to Virginia? : and other questions about the Jamestown settlement / by Candice Ransom.
      p.   cm. — (Six questions of American history)
   Includes bibliographical references and index.
   ISBN 978–0–7613–5228–0 (lib. bdg. : alk. paper)
   1. Jamestown (Va.) —History—17th century—Juvenile literature. 2. Frontier and pioneer life—Virginia—Jamestown—Juvenile literature. 3. Virginia—History—Colonial period, ca. 1600–1775—Juvenile literature. I. Title.
F234.J3R36 2011
973.2'1—dc22   2010033374

Manufactured in the United States of America
1 – DP – 12/31/10

TABLE OF CONTENTS 4

THE SIX QUESTIONS HELP YOU DISCOVER THE FACTS!

INTRODUCTION

Winter's chill wrapped around three cargo ships bobbing in the choppy English Channel. The *Susan Constant*, the *Godspeed*, and the *Discovery* had sailed from London, England, on December 20, 1606. Off the coast of Dover, England, they dropped anchor and waited for a good wind to take them across the Atlantic Ocean to North America.

Days turned into weeks. The 105 passengers and 39 sailors grew restless. Below the decks, it was cramped and dark. Dogs sighed as they curled up, trying to sleep. Chickens pecked and scratched for corn between the floorboards. Passengers listened to creaking ropes and slapping waves. They shivered in the dampness and worried about seawater leaking through the cracks.

On February 12, 1607, several passengers climbed on deck to find a clear sky. Anchors were raised, and huge canvas sails filled with a stiff wind. At last, the ships were on their way!

The English passengers came from different backgrounds, but they shared one goal—to begin a settlement in North America. They were willing to risk danger to make their hopes and dreams come true. Who were these 105 men and boys?

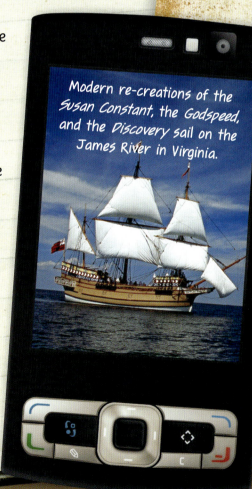

Modern re-creations of the *Susan Constant*, the *Godspeed*, and the *Discovery* sail on the James River in Virginia.

NORTH AMERICA

ATLANTIC OCEAN

SOUTH AMERICA

AFRICA

ENGLAND

IRELAND

LONDON

ENGLISH CHANNEL

DOVER

FRANCE

SPAIN

CANARY ISLANDS

WEST INDIES

CARIBBEAN SEA

N

This 1900 illustration shows English ships arriving in Virginia in 1607.

The settlers' ships cross the Atlantic Ocean in 1607 in this painting by Mike Haywood.

ONE THE GREAT ADVENTURE

The ships' passengers were part of the Virginia Company of London. The company formed in April 1606 with the permission of England's King James I. Its purpose was to send volunteers to North America. The volunteers would build a colony in a region known as Virginia.

a territory ruled by a country

The Spanish had been exploring the region since Christopher Columbus's voyage in 1492. Their

King James I of England

6

ships carried gold and silver back to Spain. England wanted to stake a claim in the riches of America. It also wanted to build colonies along the east coast of North America. Those colonies would provide bases for English ships. England could rule the Atlantic and become more powerful than Spain.

The Virginia Company wanted its colonists to find gold and silver. Colonists who brought back the precious metals would be rewarded. The company also ordered the colonists to search for a water route (such as a large river) across North America to the Pacific Ocean. At the time, Europeans did not understand how large North America was. They thought they could find an easy route to Asia by crossing North America.

The Virginia Company chose Christopher Newport to lead the voyage. Newport was famous for capturing enemy Spanish ships, and he knew the Atlantic well. The captain commanded the largest of the three ships, the *Susan Constant*.

A modern replica (exact copy) of the *Susan Constant*

Newport chose Bartholomew Gosnold to be the captain of the *Godspeed*. John Ratcliffe commanded the *Discovery*, the smallest of the ships. The council gave Newport a sealed box. Inside were the names of seven colonists who would govern the Virginia settlement.

The colonists were split into two groups based on their position in society—gentlemen and workers. Gentlemen were from important families. They did not work for a living. Instead, most gained their money and power by owning land. Gentlemen passed these family lands to their oldest sons.

But many of the gentlemen who went to Virginia were younger sons. They had no chance to inherit their family's land. Other gentlemen were military officers near the end of their careers.

Workers formed the second group. Some were laborers—workers with no special training. Some were indentured servants. Still others were farmers or crafters—workers who had special skills. Workers were needed to build the new settlement. But despite the workers' usefulness, the gentlemen looked down upon them. The gentlemen thought they had a higher position in society and were more important than the workers.

The average colonist was forty years old. Of the adults, Edward Maria Wingfield, fifty-six, was the oldest. Twenty-seven-year-old John Smith was one of the youngest. Teenagers Samuel Collier, Nathaniel Peacock, James Brumfield, and Richard Mutton also went along.

unskilled laborers who work for an employer for a fixed period of time. In exchange, the employer pays for the servant's travel, food, and housing costs.

This bronze statue of John Smith stands in Jamestown, Virginia.

The mission promised great adventure. Some men planned to make a fresh start. Most hoped to find gold and return to England in a year or two. Their job was to explore and set up a colony for England. Permanent settlers, including women, would come later.

On their voyage from England to North America, the passengers shared tight space with tools and supplies. They slept on straw mattresses on deck or in hammocks below. And they argued.

Wingfield, who held the highest rank, accused John Smith of plotting mutiny. The gentlemen did not like Smith. Smith had been in the military and was well traveled. But he was only a farmer's son—someone with no social status.

During the weeks the ships sat at anchor, the passengers and crew had eaten a lot of supplies. Soon after setting sail, Newport had to stop to buy food. The ships dropped anchor at the Canary Islands off the northwest coast of Africa.

mutiny. a rebellion against a leader, often the captain of a ship

WHO WAS JOHN SMITH?

John Smith is the most famous Jamestown settler. Born in 1580, Smith left home at sixteen to become a soldier. By the time he was twenty-five, Smith had traveled through Europe and Africa. He fought battles, sailed the Mediterranean Sea, and was captured as a slave.

Adventure was in John Smith's blood. When he learned of the Virginia Company, he signed up. Smith made many maps of the eastern part of North America and gave the name New England to the region. He died in 1631.

While there, Newport decided to arrest Smith. Smith spent the rest of the voyage in a cell aboard the *Susan Constant*.

After the ships left the Canary Islands, they sailed across the Atlantic to the West Indies.

a group of islands between the Atlantic Ocean and the Caribbean Sea, southeast of North America

The ships stopped again at some of the islands to look for food. The passengers formed parties to hunt for fresh meat. But the Englishmen were not used to the tropical heat and sun. Many fainted. Edward Brookes became the first colonist to die, probably from heatstroke.

By April 1607, the three ships had been sailing the Atlantic for almost two months. But the colonists had not yet caught sight of the Virginia coast. *Discovery*'s captain, John Ratcliffe, wanted to turn back to England. Many felt the same way.

In the silvery gleam of dawn one morning, sailors spotted land in the distance. America! The ships glided into

The English settlers row ashore in small boats while their ships lay anchored in Chesapeake Bay. This 1950s illustration is by Sidney King.

Chesapeake Bay and dropped anchor. They had arrived in Virginia.

Newport picked thirty men to go ashore in small boats. Gentlemen and trusted sailors would be the first to set foot on land. Still under arrest, John Smith watched from the ship.

NEXT QUESTION

WHERE DID THE COLONISTS BUILD THE SETTLEMENT?

John Smith talks with local Native Americans in this 1878 woodcut. The settlers met Native Americans soon after arriving in Virginia.

TWO THE NEW WORLD

The colonists knew America would be a wilderness. They would not find shops, roads, or farms. But when they landed on April 26, the colonists were pleasantly surprised by the dark green forests and refreshing streams.

Newport and his men explored the beach and woods beyond. Some were already looking for precious metals. George Percy wrote, "We could find nothing worth speaking of but fair meadows and goodly tall trees."

The men also found that they were not alone. As the colonists headed back to their ships that first evening, five Native Americans shot at them with bows and arrows.

Two colonists were wounded. The English had no idea why the Indians had attacked.

Safely back on their ships, the men began the business of forming the colony. Newport opened the sealed box from the Virginia Company. He read the names of the men chosen to lead the Virginia settlement. Wingfield, Newport, Ratcliffe, Gosnold, George Kendall, and John Martin were all gentlemen. They were shocked that John Smith's name rounded out the list. Who was Smith to share the leadership of the colony with them? Angry, the other men refused to let Smith take his position.

The box also contained instructions on building the colony. England had tried to settle in North America before, but those attempts had failed. These new instructions were meant to help the colonists avoid past mistakes.

The settlement's location was most important. The instructions said the settlement should be built 100 miles (161 kilometers) from the sea. It should be on a river with a deep harbor that could be defended from attack by enemy ships.

COMPANY RULES

The Virginia Company gave instructions to the colonists on where to build the settlement. The company also gave the settlers these rules:

- Assign twenty men to clear the ground and plant crops.
- Don't plant in marshy ground.
- Assign twenty men to build the settlement. Build the storehouse first.
- Assign forty men to look for precious metals inland and a route to the Pacific.
- Remove sails and masts from the ships to prevent anyone from escaping.
- Take care not to offend the Indians, and try to trade with them.

No Native Americans should live between the settlement and the sea. The land should have a freshwater stream and good soil. It should be clear of trees and brush.

The next day, sailors assembled the shallop. They had brought the small boat over in pieces. Newport chose a group to row across Chesapeake Bay and look for a river.

In shallow water, they found beds of oysters, some with pearls inside. On land they found a field of "fine and

a small boat with oars and sails, used in shallow waters

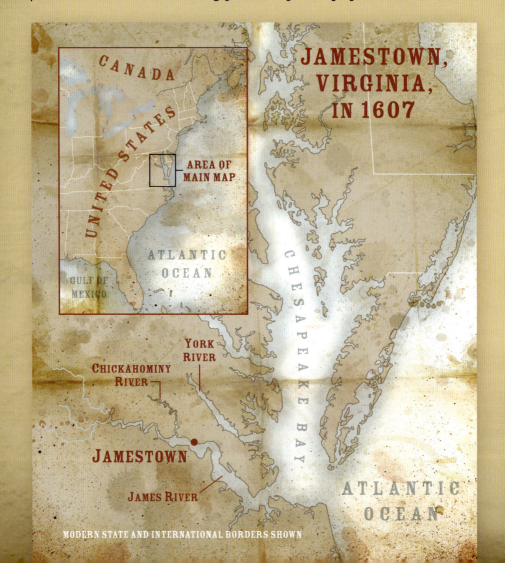

CANADA

UNITED STATES

AREA OF MAIN MAP

ATLANTIC OCEAN

GULF OF MEXICO

JAMESTOWN, VIRGINIA, IN 1607

CHESAPEAKE BAY

YORK RIVER

CHICKAHOMINY RIVER

JAMESTOWN

JAMES RIVER

ATLANTIC OCEAN

MODERN STATE AND INTERNATIONAL BORDERS SHOWN

This modern photo shows the site of early Jamestown buildings, close to the shore of the James River.

beautiful strawberries four times bigger and better than ours in England." Percy described one spot as "full of flowers . . . and as goodly trees as I have seen, as cedar, cypress, and other kinds." Virginia was the land of plenty.

The explorers then found a wide river that emptied into the Chesapeake. They named it after King James. Somewhere on the James River, they would build the colony.

On April 30, Newport and his men were greeted by five Native Americans. They were members of the Kecoughtan tribe. The Kecoughtans were part of a large group of Native Americans called the Algonquians. The Kecoughtan men led the English to their village. The colonists shared corn bread, watched a dance, and gave away glass beads. One settler, Gabriel Archer, thought the Indians looked strong and healthy compared to the tired, thin Englishmen.

After the celebration, Newport's men continued their search for a settlement site. Finding the right place was not easy. But a peninsula 30 miles (48 km) up the river had possibilities. On May 13, the explorers tied one ship to a tree on the riverbank and looked around. The harbor was deep. Thick woods could hide the settlement from enemy boats. The narrow land bridge could easily be guarded.

peninsula — an area of land jutting out into water

But the site did have some problems. The peninsula's rivers and creeks were brackish. The colonists would have to dig a well for drinking water. And the huge trees would be hard to cut down.

brackish — somewhat salty and not good for drinking

Much of the area was marshy—wetlands covered in grasses and shallow water. In summer the marshes became breeding grounds for mosquitoes. Mosquitoes carry a disease called malaria. Malaria can make humans very ill and even kill them.

WHO WERE THE ALGONQUIANS?

Most of the Native American tribes along the eastern coast of North America belonged to a group called the Algonquians. Algonquian tribes lived as far north as modern-day Canada and as far south as modern-day North Carolina. Each tribe spoke an Algonquian language.

Many Algonquian tribes on the Virginia coast belonged to a confederacy—a group that agrees to work together. Each tribe had its own leader called a werowance. The werowances were ruled by one great chief. In the early 1600s, that chief was Wahunsenacawh. He was also called Powhatan. Powhatan's confederacy included the Paspahegh, the Kecoughtan, the Arrohattoc, the Appomattoc, and the Pamunkey.

This 1880 woodcut shows the settlers making plans to begin building the colony. The colonists tried to follow the Virginia Company's rules in choosing a spot to build.

More important, the colonists didn't know that Native Americans were nearby. The Paspahegh tribe claimed the peninsula as part of their hunting territory.

The colonists knew they were going against some of the Virginia Company's rules. But they felt that they could not obey all the rules and find a perfect spot. After a heated argument, the council voted to look no more. They would build the colony on the peninsula.

NEXT QUESTION

WHY DID JOHN SMITH WANT TO BUILD A FORT?

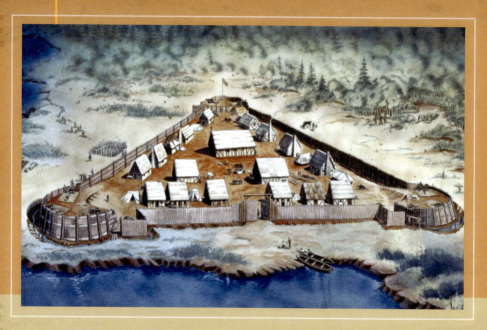

This 1950s illustration shows the Virginia settlement as it grew into Jamestown.

THREE JAMES TOWN

On May 14, the men carried provisions from the ships to the shore. John Smith pitched in even though members still would not let him join the council. They voted Wingfield as president.

Laborers, Newport's sailors, and even the gentlemen chopped down trees. Toppled trees were cut into ship's masts and boards. The lumber was loaded onto the ships to be sold in England.

Building the settlement was hard work. The colonists had only axes and hand tools. They had no horses to haul logs or to pull up tree stumps.

Members of the Paspahegh tribe came by to watch.

The Virginia Company had told the colonists to make friends with the Indians. Wingfield did not want their new neighbors to think the English did not trust them. So he would not build fortifications. Only a small fence made of tree branches circled the clearing. And most of the guns remained packed in crates.

structures, such as high walls and guard towers, built to defend a place

On May 18, one hundred Paspahegh warriors visited the settlement. It was an uneasy meeting. A fight broke out when a warrior picked up a colonist's hatchet. Angry, the Paspahegh left. But two days later, the Paspahegh returned with a deer as a peace offering.

WHERE IS THE JAMESTOWN SETTLEMENT?

Jamestown Settlement is about 60 miles (97 km) southeast of Richmond, Virginia. Two other historic sites are nearby—Colonial Williamsburg and Yorktown.

VISITING HISTORY

Colonists called the settlement James Fort and James Town. Eventually Jamestown became its name.

Jamestown Settlement is a modern attraction on the James River. Visitors can tour the re-created fort, a Powhatan village, and full-size replicas of the *Susan Constant*, the *Godspeed*, and the *Discovery*.

Historic Jamestowne, on James Island, is the site of the actual fort. Archaeologists discovered the site in 1994. You can visit the dig and view artifacts that are four hundred years old.

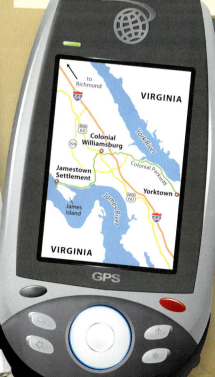

One settler asked a warrior to shoot at a target. The warrior's aim was true. The English realized that the Native Americans' simple bows and arrows weren't so primitive. Still, the settlers wanted to prove that English weapons were better. They set up a steel target. The Indian archer's arrowhead shattered against the steel. The Paspahegh again left angry.

John Smith was worried that the Paspahegh warriors would eventually attack the settlement. He asked Wingfield to let the colonists build a fort. But the council president would not listen.

A week after they landed at the settlement, Newport decided to look for the shortcut to the Pacific. He took five colonists, including Smith. Sailors made up the rest of the group. On May 21, they sailed up the James River in the shallop.

The next day, they met some Native Americans paddling a canoe. One of the Indians drew a map of the river for

In 2007 a crew set off in a replica of the 1607 shallop (left). The crew retraced John Smith's river journey as part of the four-hundredth anniversary celebration of the founding of Jamestown. In this photo, the crew pushes off from shore.

the explorers. A few days later, the Arrohattoc tribe invited the English to eat with them. The settlers learned some Algonquian words, such as *wingapoh* (good friend). They heard about the great chief Powhatan.

The English continued upriver. Along the way, they passed more villages. Native Americans offered food and made signs of friendship. The colonists reached some waterfalls (where present-day Richmond, Virginia, is located) and turned around. Rocks and shallow water made travel by boat dangerous.

When the group returned to the settlement, they were shocked at what they found. The day before, May 26, the settlers were planting corn. Suddenly about two hundred Paspahegh, Appomattoc, and other warriors attacked the colonists.

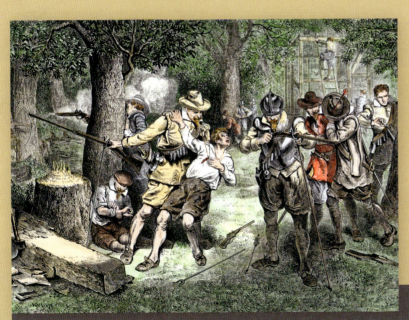

Jamestown colonists fight off a Native American attack in this 1876 woodcut. Some Native Americans were angry that the English were settling on Indian hunting lands.

With most of their guns packed in crates, the English were unarmed. One boy was killed, and at least twelve others were wounded. A second colonist later died of his wounds. The attack ended only when sailors fired cannons from the ship and frightened the attackers away.

After the attack, even Wingfield realized that the settlement needed fortifications. The men began work immediately. They built the new fort in a triangle shape. At each corner was a half-moon platform for cannons. Sturdy palisades replaced the fence.

wooden stakes sharpened at one end and bound together as a fence

As the men hammered, arrows zinged over the walls. Paspahegh warriors hid in the tall grass and fired

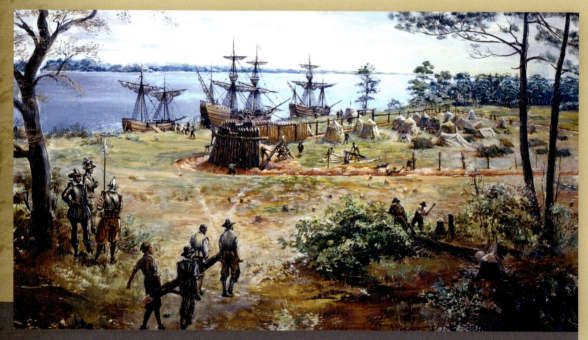

Settlers begin building James Fort in this 1956 Sidney King illustration. The fort was a triangle of tall wooden stakes surrounding the settlement's tents and buildings.

In this modern photo, a reenactor plays the role of a colonist at the Jamestown Settlement. Reenactors help visitors understand historic sites by wearing period clothing and using period tools and equipment for everyday tasks.

at the colonists. The warriors killed one settler who tried to leave the fort. The colonists saw that they should have listened to Smith's warnings. The council let him take his seat as one of the leaders of the settlement.

On June 15, the fort was finished. The settlers called it James Town, or Jamestown.

NEXT QUESTION

WHEN DID CHRISTOPHER NEWPORT LEAVE JAMESTOWN?

FOUR DEATH STALKS THE COLONY

On the morning of June 22, 1607, the *Susan Constant* and the *Godspeed* cast off and slipped down the James River. The smallest ship, the *Discovery*, was left behind for the colonists.

Captain Newport was headed back to England. His ships carried lumber and a barrel of dirt that had been dug from a stream near Jamestown. The dirt contained yellow crystals the settlers believed was gold.

Newport also carried a letter to the Virginia Company. The report described the beauty of Virginia and ended with a plea for more supplies. It was signed by the Jamestown council members.

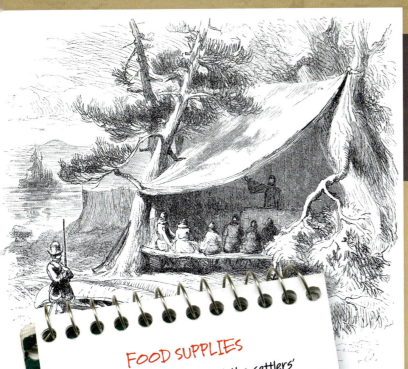

FOOD SUPPLIES

The Virginia Company stocked the settlers' ships with enough supplies for a two-month crossing and six months in America. They thought the colonists would find more food in Virginia. The settlers could trade with the Indians, plant crops, and hunt and fish.

But the crossing took nearly five months. And once in Virginia, the colonists spent all their time building and exploring. They planted corn in May but might not have tended the crop. The colonists caught fish, but they ate so much that it made them ill. Settlers hunted deer. But the hunters did not know the area well enough to follow the deer herds.

The Powhatan tribes grew corn and other vegetables. But they were not that eager to trade with the settlers. They needed their food for their own survival.

The captain had promised to return in twenty weeks with more settlers and supplies. The colonists must have felt uneasy. They were alone in a foreign land, living in tents. An old sail draped between two trees served as a church. No one knows for sure whether they built a storehouse for their food and weapons.

large freshwater fish

The river teemed with sturgeon and crabs. Raccoons, squirrels, and rabbits scurried through the woods. Yet the colonists made little attempt to fish or hunt. In his journal, Smith reported that they ate "a half a pint of wheat, and as much barley boiled with water for one man a day—and this contained as many worms as grains."

The colonists quit working on the fort too. They drifted along without real purpose. Smith blamed the lack of energy on too much hard work in the hot sun.

Then tragedy struck. On August 6, settler John Asbie died of illness.

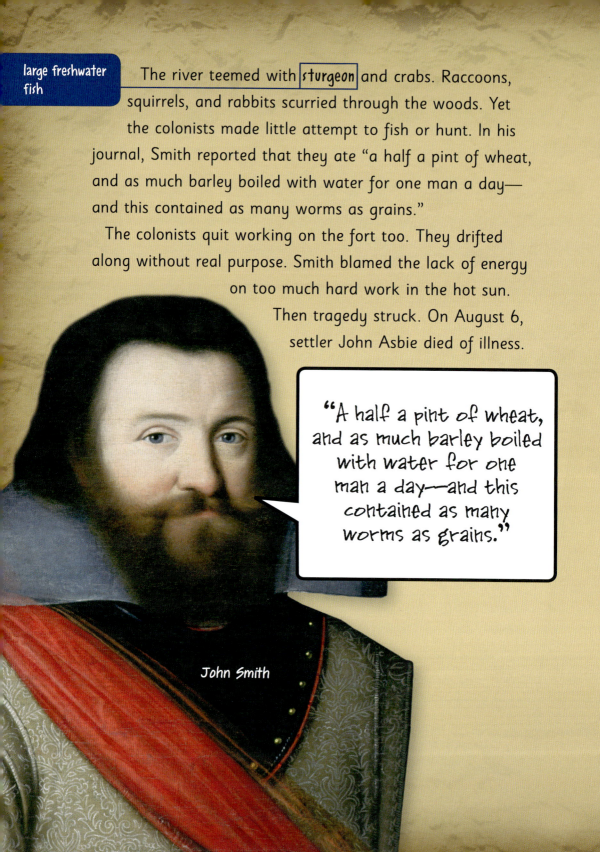

"A half a pint of wheat, and as much barley boiled with water for one man a day—and this contained as many worms as grains."

John Smith

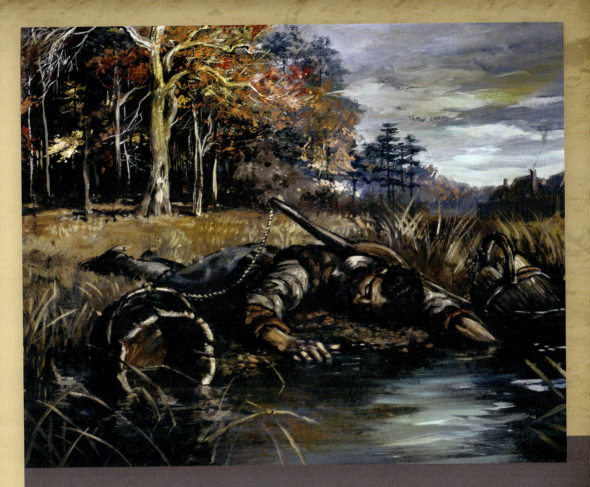

A settler fetching water falls down from exhaustion and hunger in this 1950s illustration by Sidney King. Many Jamestown colonists fell ill in the summer of 1607.

Three days later, George Flower was dead. The next day, William Brewster died.

The death toll grew from one man every few days to two or three a night. George Percy recorded the grim list. "The eighteenth day," he wrote, "there died Robert Pennington, and John Martin." The colonists died of mysterious swellings, fevers, fluxes, and infections.

excess fluids flowing from the body, such as sweat or blood

Only five men were able to stand guard at any given time. The rest of the colonists groaned "in every corner of the fort, most pitiful to hear," Percy wrote. Smith fell ill but recovered. Survivors buried the dead quietly.

The men suspected the water made them sick. Percy wrote that the water was salty at high tide and "full of slime and filth" at low tide. No one knows why they did not search for freshwater or boil the river water.

One man did not get sick—Edward Wingfield. Smith accused the council president of hoarding food. Smith said Wingfield gave the settlers wormy barley but kept chicken, eggs, oatmeal, and wine for himself and his friends.

On September 10, Smith, John Martin, and John Ratcliffe fired Wingfield from the council. Ratcliffe took Wingfield's place as

collecting and storing items, often secretly

"[The water] is full of slime and filth."

George Percy

In this 2005 photo, a chicken walks in front of the fireplace at a house in the historic Jamestown Settlement.

president. He put Smith in charge of trading with the Native Americans for corn. Colder weather was coming. The colony only had enough food for a few weeks. It was up to Smith to save Jamestown.

NEXT QUESTION

WHAT DID THE NATIVE AMERICANS DO WHEN JOHN SMITH ASKED FOR CORN?

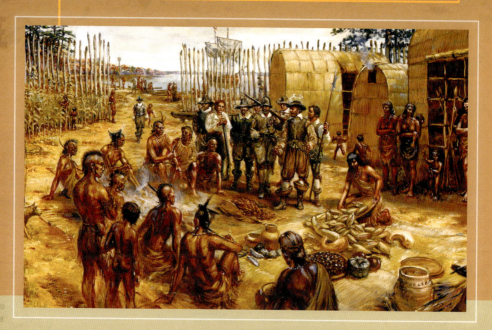

John Ratcliffe put John Smith in charge of trading for food with Native Americans. This 1950s illustration shows Smith trying to bargain for corn with Native American villagers.

FIVE SMITH TAKES CHARGE

Smith glanced over the sick and weak colonists. He knew he had to do something. Smith gathered six or seven of the strongest men. The group set off in the shallop, rowing downriver to the Kecoughtan village.

At the village, the Kecoughtans offered the colonists "a handful of corn" in return for their guns. Smith knew that he and his men looked ragged and starved—in no position to bargain. He had to show the Kecoughtans that the English were not weak.

Smith ordered his men to fire their guns into the air. The Kecoughtans ran into the woods. In their village, Smith found piles of corn. A Native American priest came out of a hut, making signs of peace. Smith offered to trade beads for food. The Kecoughtan villagers then returned. They loaded the shallop with deer meat and corn.

Back at Jamestown, the colonists ate greedily. But Smith knew the corn would only last four or five days. Ratcliffe volunteered to take the *Discovery* back to England to get supplies. But Smith suspected that Ratcliffe would never return. Instead, Smith decided to take both the *Discovery* and the shallop up the James River. His goal was to get as much food as possible, taking it from the Native American villagers if necessary.

On November 9, 1607, Smith and a crew of eight men took the shallop to explore the Chickahominy River. They would meet up with the seven-man crew of the *Discovery* later, 20 miles (32 km) upriver.

This modern photo shows the Chickahominy River with bald cypress, pines, and wild rice along the shoreline.

Smith stopped at several villages. The Native Americans treated the English kindly. Smith was able to trade for fifty bushels of corn. He learned new Algonquian words so he could talk to the villagers.

In the late fall, the weather turned cold. The settlers hunted migrating geese and ducks. That gave them enough food for a while.

Smith decided to finish exploring the Chickahominy River. He may have wanted to find the water route to the Pacific Ocean. In early December, he left in the shallop with Thomas Emry, John Robinson, George Cassen, and six other men.

After 50 miles (80 km), the river became narrow and shallow. Smith was afraid of wrecking the shallop. He asked two Indians from a nearby village to take a small party upriver in a canoe. He said the party wanted to hunt for birds. Smith, Emry, and Robinson climbed into the canoe. Smith ordered the rest of his crew to stay behind on the shallop.

The Native Americans did not believe Smith's story. Why would the English travel 50 miles (80 km) up the Chickahominy when there were plenty of birds on the James River? After Smith left, the warriors in the village headed for the shallop. They attacked the men Smith had left behind. George Cassen was captured and killed.

The party in the canoe had no idea what was happening at the shallop. Smith and his crew paddled upriver and then stopped to make camp. With one of the guides, Smith went into the woods to hunt for game. A few minutes later, he

heard a cry from the camp. Then an arrow grazed Smith's thigh.

Smith reacted quickly. He pushed his guide in front of him as a shield. Smith dragged the guide along, heading for the shallop. But he slipped in the mud and was caught. Smith surrendered. The Indians took him to the Pamunkey werowance, Opechancanough.

Opechancanough was Powhatan's younger brother. He was second in line to take over Powhatan's kingdom. Opechancanough did not trust the English.

Smith had to think fast. His life was at stake.

NEXT QUESTION

WHO WAS POCAHONTAS?

SIX AMONG THE POWHATANS

a device that shows directions— north, south, east, and west

Smith took out his ivory compass. He told Opechancanough that the earth was round, not flat, and that it revolved around the sun. He described boundless oceans and vast countries where men of many nations lived.

Opechancanough seemed interested. He tried to touch the moving needles through the glass. Smith hoped the chief believed Smith was the leader of the English. The Algonquian tribes respected leaders.

His plan worked. He was led to the Pamunkey hunting lodges, where he stayed several days. He was fed deer meat and bread. Opechancanough asked him about the fort's cannons. Smith suspected the werowance was planning an attack.

Smith ripped a sheet from his writing tablet and wrote a warning to the colonists in Jamestown. He told them to fire their guns as a show of power and to send back items he listed. Three messengers left with Smith's letter. They came back with the things Smith had requested. The Pamunkeys, who had no written language, were amazed by "paper that talked."

On December 30, Pamunkey warriors took Smith to Werowocomoco, Powhatan's village. No Englishman had ever seen the great chief. Smith waited nervously outside the chief's lodge while two hundred warriors stared at him. Finally, he was led inside.

Powhatan sat on a low bed before a fire. The gray-haired chief wore a robe of raccoon skins and long pearl necklaces. Powhatan's sister, Opossunoquonuske, brought Smith water to wash his hands. Then the women and girls served the men a feast.

POWHATAN

Wahunsenacawh, or Powhatan, was probably born in the late 1540s, near present-day Richmond, Virginia. His village was called Powhatan. Wahunsenacawh became the leader of the village and took its name as his own. He also became the leader of six other tribes. By the early 1600s, Powhatan ruled about seventy-five thousand people in thirty tribes.

When the settlers arrived, Powhatan was in his sixties. He did not trust the English. But Powhatan tried to exist peacefully with the colonists. He saw that their guns could protect his kingdom from his enemies. Powhatan died in April 1618.

A Coniurer.   Their   Idoll   A Preist

Their Coniuration about C: Smith 1607

With Algonquian words and hand signals, Powhatan asked Smith why the English had come. Smith realized this was not a good time to say they were there to stay. Using the few native words he knew, he told Powhatan that the English had been chased into Chesapeake Bay by Spanish ships. The English had built a fort while they repaired their leaking boat. They would go back across the ocean when Newport came with supplies.

Then Powhatan wanted to know why the English had sailed so far upriver. Smith said they were looking for a great sea to the west. That, at least, was true.

What happened next is one of Jamestown's most puzzling events. Many years after he had left Jamestown, Smith wrote that Powhatan ordered two stones brought into the lodge. Smith was forced to lay his head on the top rock. Warriors stood over him with clubs, ready to bash his skull.

Then a young girl ran over and laid her head on top of Smith's. She was Pocahontas, Powhatan's daughter. Smith said she begged her father to spare Smith's life. Powhatan agreed. Why did Powhatan threaten to kill Smith and then treat him as a friend? Some historians think Smith was part of a ceremony. Powhatan's warriors pretended to kill the old Smith so a new Smith could be adopted into the tribe as Powhatan's son. Pocahontas may have been acting her part in the ceremony.

This print, published by Henry Schile in 1870, shows Pocahontas leaning over John Smith, preventing Opechancanough from striking him. Powhatan is standing behind Smith.

POCAHONTAS

Pocahontas was born in about 1595. She was about eleven years old when John Smith came to her village. No one is sure what real role she played in rescuing Smith from death. But Smith wrote that she also brought food to Jamestown after the January fire. Her gift of food, Smith said, saved many lives.

On April 5, 1614, Pocahontas married colonist John Rolfe. Later, she sailed to England with Rolfe and their baby, Thomas. In 1617, at the age of twenty-one, Pocahontas died of an unknown illness. She was buried in England.

On Saturday, January 2, 1608, Smith arrived back in Jamestown with several of Powhatan's men. Smith had promised to send the chief two cannons and a millstone.

> a circular stone used to grind wheat and other grains into flour

The Indians were unable to carry the cannons or the millstone without equipment. Smith knew this when he made the promise. Instead, he gave the men beads and bells.

Smith found the fort was in a state of confusion. The settlers could not fish in the frozen river, and food supplies were low again. Several settlers had boarded the *Discovery* and were threatening to leave. Smith ordered cannons aimed at the ship until the deserters got off and returned to the fort.

> people who leave a place without permission

But Smith's troubles were not over. While Smith had been captive, some members of his crew had found their way back to the settlement. They gave the news that Smith had disappeared. The colonists had formed a search party. They didn't find Smith. But they did bring back the bodies of Emry and Robinson, both dead from arrows. The council blamed Smith for the deaths of his men. The council decided that Smith would be hung the next day.

But before Smith could be hung, a ship appeared on the river. Christopher Newport had returned in the *John and Francis*. He brought sixty new colonists and much-needed supplies. Overjoyed at the sight of fresh potatoes, pineapples, and bananas, the colonists freed Smith.

On Monday the new colonists moved into the fort. A few days later, on January 7, fire spread through Jamestown. No one was hurt, but huts and supplies were destroyed. It was another bad blow for the settlement. But the colonists picked up their axes and began rebuilding.

In September 1608, Smith was elected president of the colony. In October, 70 new colonists arrived, including the first two women. In 1609, 450 more colonists came to Jamestown.

This photo shows the inside of a replica Powhatan home at the Jamestown Settlement historic site in Virginia. The site's Powhatan village includes houses and crops.

Smith returned to England after being seriously injured in an explosion.

Later that year, supply ships bound for Jamestown were lost in a storm. The winter of 1609 and 1610 became known as the Starving Time. Out of five hundred colonists, only sixty survived.

In 1610 King James I provided stronger leadership and protection for Jamestown. He sent a governor and military troops. But the colony still struggled to make money and trade food. Then, in 1613, colonist John Rolfe planted tobacco. Tobacco became a successful cash crop for the colony. Jamestown grew fast.

a crop sold to make money

This 1950s illustration by Sidney King shows Jamestown colonists after a winter storm.

THE FIRST AFRICANS IN JAMESTOWN

In 1619 English pirates raided a Portuguese slave ship. The English ship brought more than twenty Africans to Jamestown and traded them for supplies. The Africans worked as indentured servants. They were the first Africans to live in Virginia.

In 1624 Virginia became a royal colony. It was ruled by the English government and no longer owned by the Virginia Company. Jamestown was the center of the colony's government until 1699. Then the capital moved to the new town of Williamsburg. By the mid-1700s, the town of Jamestown was abandoned and taken over by large farms. But Jamestown kept its place in history as the first permanent English colony in North America.

NEXT QUESTION

HOW DO WE KNOW ABOUT LIFE IN JAMESTOWN?

Primary Source: John Smith's Writings

The best way to learn about any historical event is with primary sources. Primary sources are created near the time being studied. They include diaries or journals, letters, newspaper articles, documents, speeches, pamphlets, photos, paintings, and other items. They are made by people who have firsthand knowledge of the event.

John Smith published several books about his life and Jamestown. Smith's *A True Relation of Such Occurrences and Accident of Note as Happened in Virginia* was published in 1608. Later, Smith wrote *A Map of Virginia, with a Description of the Country and the Proceedings of the English Colony in America*. Both were published in 1612, three years after his return to England. In his book, *The General History of Virginia, New England, and the Summer Isles*, Smith describes how Pocahontas saved his life.

Historians believe parts of Smith's books were copied from other colonists' writings. But his colorful descriptions help us see life in Jamestown and early Virginia. In *A True Relation*, Smith writes:

> Our provision [food] now being within twenty days spent, the Indians brought us great store of both corn and bread ready-made. And also there came such abundance of fowls into the rivers as greatly refreshed our weak estates [condition], whereupon many of our weak men were presently able to go abroad [move around].
>
> As yet we had no houses to cover us, our tents were rotten, and our cabins worse than nought [nothing].

TELL YOUR JAMESTOWN STORY

You are a settler who has just arrived in Virginia. North America is so different from your old home in England. Write a journal entry or a letter back home describing your experiences.

WHO are you? (Are you a boy, girl, man, or woman?)

WHERE did you live originally?

WHY have you come to Virginia?

WHEN did you arrive?

WHAT is the most astonishing thing about North America?

HOW do you get along with the other settlers?

HOW do you get along with the Native Americans?

USE **WHO, WHAT, WHERE WHY, WHEN,** AND **HOW** TO THINK OF OTHER QUESTIONS TO HELP YOU CREATE YOUR STORY!

Timeline

1606

England's King James I grants a charter to the Virginia Company to set up a colony in North America.

The *Susan Constant*, the *Discovery*, and the *Godspeed* leave England with 105 colonists.

1607

In April the ships arrived in the Chesapeake Bay.

In May the colonists decide to build their settlement on a peninsula. The new settlement is attacked by Paspahegh warriors.

In June colonists finish building a fort. Christopher Newport sails back to England.

Later that summer, almost half the colonists die from fevers and other illnesses. John Smith begins trading for corn with the Native Americans.

In December Smith is captured and taken to meet the great leader Powhatan. Later, Smith will claim that **Powhatan's daughter Pocahontas saved him from death.**

1608

In January Smith returns to Jamestown. Newport returns from England with supplies and new settlers. A fire destroys most of Jamestown.

In April Newport sails back to England. A second supply ship brings forty new settlers to Jamestown.

1608 (continued)

Smith leaves Jamestown in June to explore the Chesapeake Bay.

In September the Jamestown council elects Smith as president.

In October Newport arrives in Jamestown with new colonists, including two women.

1609

In August 450 new colonists arrive in Jamestown.

Smith leaves for England in September.

1610

In January and February, **many colonists die of starvation.**

In May ships arrive to find only sixty colonists alive.

1618

Powhatan dies.

1619

More than twenty Africans are brought to Jamestown as indentured servants.

1624

Virginia becomes a royal colony with Jamestown as its capital.

1631

John Smith dies in London at the age of 51.

1699

The capital of Virginia moves from Jamestown to Williamsburg.

SOURCE NOTES

12 Benjamin Woolley, *Savage Kingdom: The True Story of Jamestown, 1607, and the Settlement of America* (New York: HarperCollins, 2007), 56.

14–15 Ibid., 58.

15 Ibid.

26 John M. Thompson, ed., *The Journals of Captain John Smith* (Washington, DC: National Geographic, 2007), 11.

27 David A. Price, *Love and Hate in Jamestown: John Smith, Pocahontas, and the Heart of a New Nation* (New York: Knopf, 2003), 49.

28 Ivor Noel Hume, *The Virginia Adventure: Roanoke to James Town, an Archaeological and Historical Odyssey* (New York: Knopf, 1994), 159.

28 Price, *Love and Hate in Jamestown*, 48.

35 Hume, *The Virginia Adventure*, 177.

42 Edward Wright Haile, *Jamestown Narratives, Eyewitness Accounts of the Virginia Colony, the First Decade: 1607–1617* (Champlain, VA: Round House, 1998), 149.

SELECTED BIBLIOGRAPHY

Horn, James. *A Land as God Made It: Jamestown and the Birth of America.* New York: Basic Books, 2005.

Kelso, William M. *Jamestown: The Buried Truth.* Charlottesville: University of Virginia Press, 2006.

Loker, Aleck. *Fearless Captain: The Adventures of John Smith.* Greensboro, NC: Morgan Reynolds, 2006.

Price, David A. *Love and Hate in Jamestown: John Smith, Pocahontas, and the Heart of a New Nation.* New York: Knopf, 2003.

Rountree, Helen C. *Pocahontas, Powhatan, Opechancanough: Three Indians Lives Changed by Jamestown.* Charlottesville: University of Virginia, 2005.

Southern, Ed, ed. *The Jamestown Adventure: Accounts of the Virginia Colony, 1605–1614.* Winston-Salem, NC: John Blair, 2004.

Thompson, John M., ed. *The Journals of Captain John Smith.* Washington, DC: National Geographic, 2007.

FURTHER READING AND WEBSITES

Fritz, Jean. *The Double Life of Pocahontas*. New York: Putnam, 2002. This book tells the true story of Pocahontas and her important role in the Jamestown colony.

Jamestown
http://cybersleuthkids.com/sleuth/History/US_History/Colonial_Period/Jamestown/index.htm
This CyberSleuth Kids site includes links to lots of information about Jamestown, including maps and photographs.

Jamestown Settlement
http://www.historyisfun.org/Jamestown-Settlement.htm
The main website of the living history museum of Jamestown has photos of a re-created Powhatan village, the *Susan Constant*, the *Godspeed*, and the *Discovery* ships. A timeline of events that happened in Jamestown is included.

Karwoski, Gail. *Miracle: The True Story of the Wreck of the* Sea Venture. Minneapolis: Millbrook Press, 2004. A thrilling account of a ship bound for Jamestown that is lost in a storm. Survivors live on an island, build smaller ships, and eventually make it to Jamestown in time to save the starving colonists.

Lange, Karen. *1607: A New Look at Jamestown*. Washington, DC: National Geographic, 2007. Using photographs and a lively text, this book describes the discovery of the original Jamestown fort in 1994. Archaeological findings show how women, indentured servants, and Native Americans changed the settlement.

On the Trail of Captain John Smith: A Jamestown Adventure
http://kids.nationalgeographic.com/kids/games/interactiveadventures/john-smith
Based on the book *John Smith Escapes Again!*, this website narrates the story of Jamestown, with games such as building the fort, a treasure hunt, and a boat race.

Rosen, Daniel. *Jamestown and the Virginia Colony 1607–1699*. Washington, DC: National Geographic, 2005. This book covers the history of the first Jamestown colony through the creation of Williamsburg. Interesting facts are illustrated with color photographs and paintings.

Schanzer, Rosalyn. *John Smith Escapes Again!* Washington, DC: National Geographic, 2006. Cartoon illustrations and a fun narrative show that Captain John Smith had many adventures before and after the founding of Jamestown. Based on Smith's own writings, the book backs up facts with maps, illustrated sidebars, and a detailed author's note.

Walker, Sally M. *Written in Bone: Buried Lives of Jamestown and Colonial Maryland*. Minneapolis: Carolrhoda Books, 2009. Follow the exciting investigations of scientists who use detective work to learn about people buried near Jamestown and other colonial sites.

Index

Photo Acknowledgments

The images in this book are used with the permission of: © hilmi/Shutterstock Images, textured wall backgrounds used throughout; © iStockphoto.com/DNY59, p. 1; © iStockphoto.com/sx70, p. 3 (top), 10, 13, 16, 19 (top), 25 (bottom), 35, 38, 41 (top); © iStockphoto.com/Ayse Nazli Deliormanli, PDA on pp. 3, 43; © iStockphoto.com/Serdar Yagci, pp. 4–5 (background), 43 (background); © iStockphoto .com/Andrey Pustovoy, smart phone on pp. 4, 7, 9, 15, 20, 23, 29, 31, 39; © Bill Hauser/Independent Picture Service, pp. 4–5 (map); © Visions of America/Alamy, p. 4 (inset); © Time Life Pictures/Mansell/ Getty Images, pp. 5 (bottom), 44; © Mike Haywood, p. 6 (top); © John Decritz the Elder/Bridgeman Art Library/Getty Images, p. 6 (bottom); © Ed George/National Geographic/Getty Images, p. 7 (inset); © Thomas J. Abercrombie/National Geographic/Getty Images, p. 9 (inset); Courtesy National Park Service, Colonial National Historical Park, pp. 11, 22, 27, 30, 40, 45; © North Wind Picture Archives, pp. 12, 17, 21, 34; © Laura Westlund and Bill Hauser/Independent Picture Service, p. 14; © Ira Block/ National Geographic/Getty Images, p. 15 (inset), 23 (inset), 29 (inset); © MPI/Stringer/Getty Images, p. 18; © iStockphoto.com/Talshiar, p. 19 (GPS); © Laura Westlund/Independent Picture Service, p. 19 (map); AP Photo/Gary C. Knapp, p. 20 (inset); Mary Evans Picture Library/Everett Collection, p. 24; The Granger Collection, New York, p. 25 (top); English School, 17th century/Private Collection/The Bridgeman Art Library, p. 26; © Archive Photos/Stringer/Getty Images, p. 28; © Susan M. Glascock, p. 31 (inset); The Beinecke Rare Book and Manuscript Library, Yale University, pp. 33, 36; Library of Congress (LC-USZ62-17680), p. 37; © Natalie Tepper/Arcaid/Alamy, p. 39 (inset); © Richard Schlecht/ National Geographic/Getty Images, p. 43 (painting).

Front cover: Painting by Sydney King, courtesy National Park Service, Colonial National Historical Park. Back cover: © hilmi/Shutterstock Images.